Table of Contents

Module 1 1

Module 2 3

Module 3 6

Module 4 7

Module 5 13

Module 6 15

Module 7 21

Module 8 23

Module 9 25

Module 10 30

Module 11 32

Module 12 36

Module 13 39

Module 14 42

Module 15 46

Module 16 50

Module 17 58

Module 18 65

This workbook contains all of the worksheets that can be found in the Science Kindergarten A course. Students are expected to submit all completed work to his or her teacher.

© 2021 by Accelerate Education
Visit us on the Web at www.accelerate.education

SCIENCE

The Summer Season Assignment

Name: _____

1. In the box below, draw one or more pictures of your favorite things about summer. You can draw on a separate piece of paper and glue inside the box.

Draw or glue

1
1.1 The Summer Season Next Page

2. Glue your pressed flowers in the box below.

1.1 The Summer Season

Leaves and Butterflies Assignment

Name: _____

1. In the box below, draw a picture of what you saw in the trees.

Draw

3

2.1 Leaves and Butterflies Next Page

2. Draw a picture of the life cycle of the butterfly in the box below.

Draw

2.1 Leaves and Butterflies

3. Glue your leaf rubbing picture in the box below.

SCIENCE

Deer in Fall Assignment

Name: _____

1. In the box below, draw a picture of a buck, a doe, or a fawn.

Draw

3.1 Deer in Fall

Autumn Leaves and Weather Conditions

Name: _____

1. In the box below, draw a picture of the leaves you collected and label the tree that each leaf comes from.

Draw

4.1 Autumn Leaves and Weather Conditions Next Page

2. Glue your leaves onto the boxes below, sorting them by size and color.

Size: _____

Color: _____   Glue

Size: _____

Color: _____   Glue

Size: _____

Color: _____   Glue

Size: _____

Color: _____   Glue

4.1 Autumn Leaves and Weather Conditions

3. Make observations about the weather on a sunny day. Set up an umbrella or a tent to reduce the sunlight on sand, soil, rocks, and water. List your observations below.

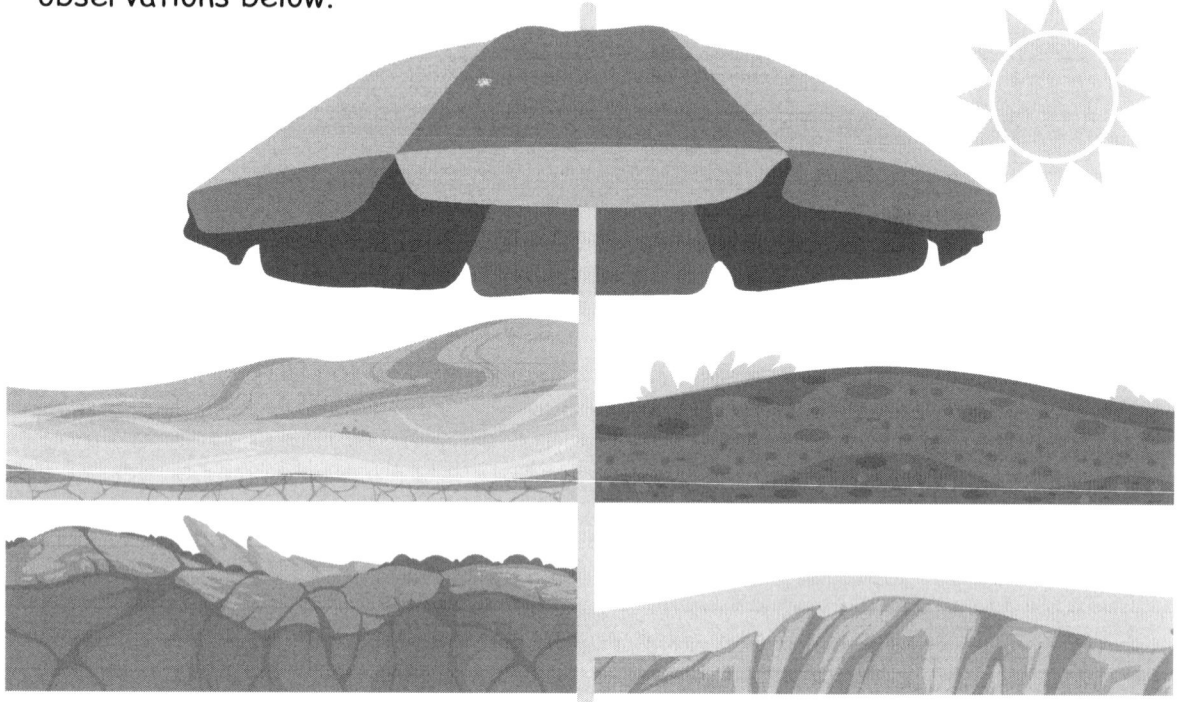

Cooler or warmer to the touch in shade

_____

_____

_____

_____

_____

_____

_____

_____

4. Glue the leaves you pressed in the box below.

Making a Weather Chart

Name: _____

1. On the chart below record the wind direction, the temperature, and the time the sun sets each day.

Weather Chart

Wind direction	Temperature	Sun Setting

2. Go outside each night and look at the sky. Depending on what you see, predict what the weather will be the next day. Are you correct (yes or no)?

Predict the Weather

Cloudy or Clear	Predict Tomorrow's Weather	Yes or No

3. Draw a picture of the Wind Vane you made.

Draw

4.2 Making a Weather Chart

SCIENCE

Autumn and Falling Leaves

Name: _____

1. In the box below, draw a picture of a tree with leaves falling.

Draw

13   5.1 Autumn and Falling Leaves Next Page

2. In the box below, draw a picture of your special tree and label what it is.

My Special Tree!

Draw

5.1 Autumn and Falling Leaves

SCIENCE

Squirrel Behavior Assignment

Name: _____

1. In the box below, draw a picture of a squirrel gathering nuts or scampering up a tree.

Draw

15   6.1 Squirrel Behavior Next Page

2. Name two things squirrels do to get ready for the winter.

3. Where do squirrels live in the winter?

4. What happens if a squirrel doesn't eat some of the tree seeds or nuts they buried?

5. Draw a picture of the squirrels you watched.

Draw

6. What was the weather like the day you watched the squirrels?

6.1 Squirrel Behavior

SCIENCE

Animal Habitat and Weather

Name: _____

1. In the box below, draw a picture of animal homes you found this week. Label the animals and types of homes you found. Describe where they live.

Draw

6.2 Animal Habitats and Weather

2. What kinds of animals live underground?

3. What kinds of animals live in trees? Why?

4. How do some termites build their nests twenty feet tall?

5. What kinds of animals dwell in caves?

6. Where do beavers build their homes and how do they do so?

SCIENCE

Duck Observations

Name: _____

1. In the box below, draw a picture of a baby duck. You can use your imagination plus what you learned in this lesson.

Draw

7.1 Duck Observation Next Page

2. What does the word "**duck**" mean?

3. What is a flyway?

4. Why do some birds fly south for the winter?

7.1 Duck Observation

Natural Fall Objects

Name: _____

1. Find many signs of fall in your nature walk and list them in the box below.

Signs of Fall
(List what you found!)

2. In the box below, draw a picture of some of the objects you gathered on your walk. Play your memory game with them.

Draw

8.1 Natural Fall Objects

SCIENCE

Observing Nature

Name: _____

1. In the boxes below, draw a picture of some of the wonderful objects you examined with your magnifying glass. Label and classify them in each box.

Object

[_____]

rough/smooth _____

hard/soft _____

large/small _____

heavy/light _____

Draw

Object

[_____]

rough/smooth _____

hard/soft _____

large/small _____

heavy/light _____

Draw

9.1 Observing Nature Next Page

Continue to label and classify your objects.

Object

[ ]

rough/smooth _____

hard/soft _____

large/small _____

heavy/light _____

Draw

Object

[ ]

rough/smooth _____

hard/soft _____

large/small _____

heavy/light _____

Draw

9.1 Observing Nature

Continue to label and classify your objects.

Object

[   ]

rough/smooth _____

hard/soft _____

large/small _____

heavy/light _____

Draw

Object

[   ]

rough/smooth _____

hard/soft _____

large/small _____

heavy/light _____

Draw

9.1 Observing Nature

2. Make up a story about life in the miniature world you saw through your magnifying glass. Write your story below and draw a picture about it on the next page.

3. Draw a picture of your miniature world story.

Draw

SCIENCE

Animal Camouflage

Name: _____

1. In the box below, draw a picture of an animal using animal camouflage (a way of hiding) during a season. Label the animal and the season.

Animal _____   Season _____

Draw

10.1 Animal Camouflage

30 Next Page

2. Why do animals use camouflage?

_____
_____
_____
_____
_____
_____

3. What animals are active where you live during the winter? Do they change color?

_____
_____
_____
_____
_____
_____

4. Keep track of weather conditions this week by filling out the chart below.

Weekly Weather Chart

Wind Direction	Temperature	Sun/Clouds/Rain

SCIENCE

Listening to Nature

Name: _____

1. Listen for the many different sounds of nature. List what you heard in the box below.

Sounds of Nature
(List what you heard!)

_____   _____

_____   _____

_____   _____

_____   _____

_____   _____

_____   _____

_____   _____

11.1 Listening to Nature

2. Make up stories about what the birds may be saying to each other and write the stories on the lines below.

3. Draw a picture of your story.

4. Listen for the many different sounds you hear at night. List what you heard on the lines below.

The Sounds at Night
(List what you heard at night!)

11.1 Listening to Nature

SCIENCE

Nature Review

Name: _____

1. Below and on the next pages, draw what you learned about the fall season. You can also cut out pictures and glue them into the boxes. Label your pictures.

_____

Draw or glue

_____

Draw or glue

12.1 Nature Review

36 Next Page

Draw or glue

Draw or glue

Draw or glue

37 12.1 Nature Review Next Page

12.1 Nature Review

SCIENCE

Plant a Garden

Name: _____

1. In the box below, draw a picture of plants growing in soil.

Draw

39

13.1 Plant a Garden Next Page

2. Plant indoor gardens and observe them throughout the coming months. Start your plant experiment this week by growing an avocado or sweet potato in water. Record your **weekly** plant growth below.

Weekly Plant Journal

Day	Record the Progress	Draw the Progress

13.1 Plant a Garden

3. What do plants need to grow?

Forces Observation Chart

Name: _____

I exerted a force on something when I . . .	Something around me exerted a force on something else when . . .

SCIENCE

Assemble and Plant a Terrarium

Name: _____

1. In the box below, draw a picture of the terrarium you planted.

Draw

43   14.2 Assemble and Plant a Terrarium Next Page

2. Continue recording your plant growth experiment this week with an avocado or sweet potato in water.

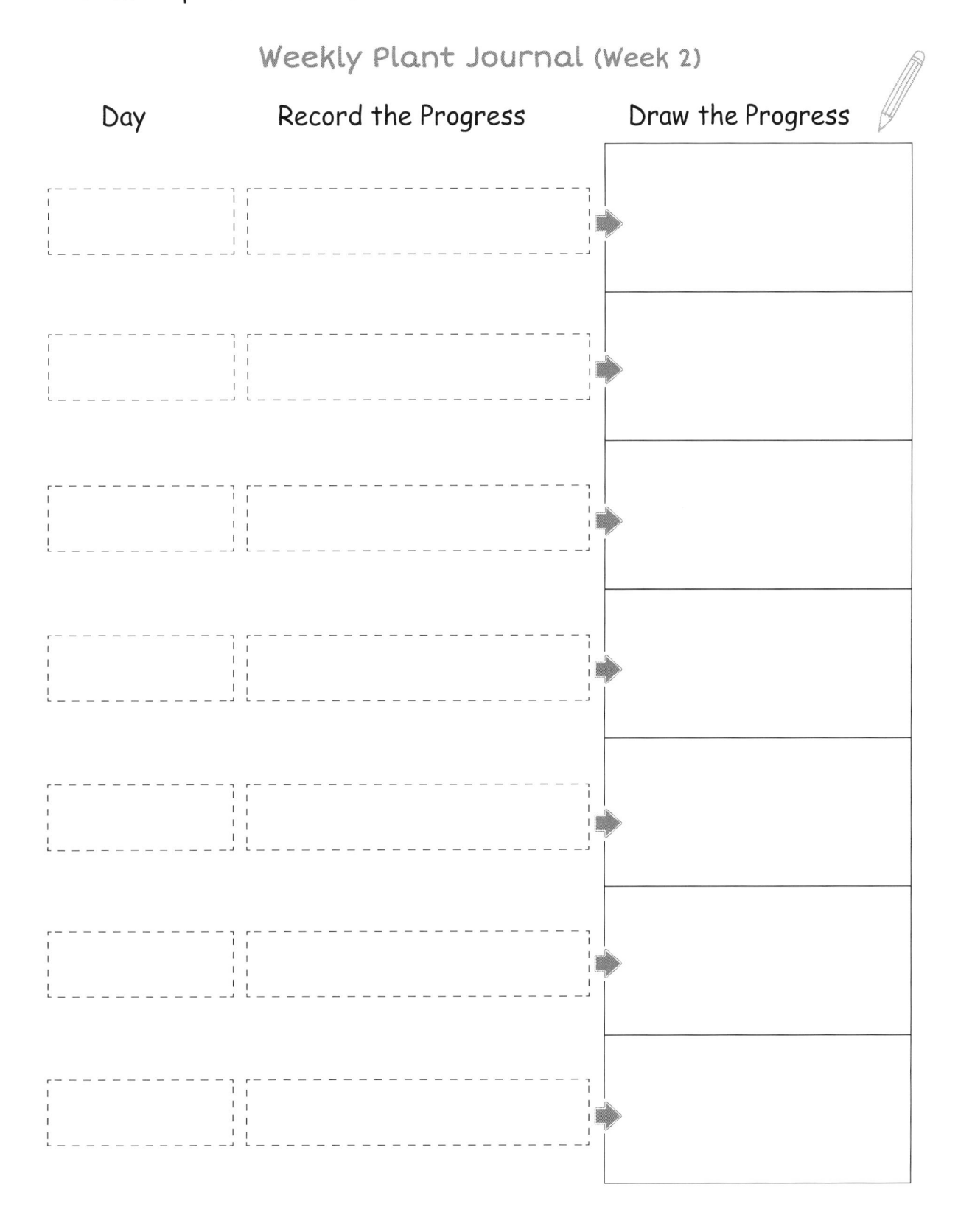

Weekly Plant Journal (Week 2)

Day	Record the Progress	Draw the Progress

14.2 Assemble and Plant a Terrarium

3. Why do you think the terrarium jar should be sealed with the plastic?

_____
_____
_____
_____
_____

4. Has anything changed since you first visited your special tree?

_____
_____
_____
_____
_____

SCIENCE

Movement Brainstorming

Name: _____

Add your own words to describe how you move!

- whirl
- jump
- spin
- dash

15.1 Motion

SCIENCE

Observing Motion

Name: _____

Directions: Use the photo of the girl and the balloons to complete this worksheet.

1. Circle the word that completes the sentence.

    a. The girl is _____ the ground.   **above**   **below**

    b. The balloons are _____ the girl.   **in front of**   **behind**

    c. The grass is _____ the girl.   **in front of**   **behind**

2. Is the girl's position changing?
   _____
   _____
   _____

3. Circle the words that describe a motion.

    roll   **slide**   **push**   **pull**

    spin   **force**   **bounce**   **feet**

4. Which of the objects in the photo are moving on their own? Which objects are being pushed or pulled by something?

Objects That Are Moving on Their Own	Objects That Are Being Pushed or Pulled

15.1 Motion

SCIENCE

Grow a Bean Seed

Name: _____

1. In the box below, draw a picture of your bean seed sprouting and answer the question below it. On the next page, continue recording your avocado/sweet potato experiment findings.

[Draw]

2. Observe the growth of the seeds and describe how the roots, stems and leaves start to grow.

_____
_____
_____
_____
_____

15.2 Grow a Bean Seed

48 Next Page

3. Continue recording your plant growth experiment this week with an avocado or sweet potato in water.

Weekly Plant Journal (Week 3)

Day	Record the Progress	Draw the Progress

15.2 Grow a Bean Seed

SCIENCE

Make a Goldfish Bowl

Name: _____

1. Check on the progress of your indoor planting experiments. In the box below, draw a picture of the terrarium as it looks now.

Draw

2. How is your terrarium doing? Are the plants thriving or struggling?

_____
_____
_____
_____

16.1 Make a Goldfish Bowl

3. Continue recording your plant growth experiment this week with an avocado or sweet potato in water.

Weekly Plant Journal (Week ___)

Day	Record the Progress	Draw the Progress

4. Assemble your goldfish bowl and draw a picture of it below.

Draw

5. What do fish need to live?

16.1 Make a Goldfish Bowl

6. In the box below, draw different fish that you learned about. Label the parts of a fish.

Draw

SCIENCE

Freezing Water and Magnets

Name: _____

1. Find a puddle of water and watch it periodically during a 24-hour period to see if it turns to ice. In the box below, draw a picture of the puddle and answer questions.

[Draw]

Use a thermometer

2. What is the outside temperature when the puddle is still liquid.

_____

_____

3. What is the outside temperature when the puddle has turned to ice. (If it hasn't turned to ice, look up the temperature on the internet to find out the temperature water freezes.)

_____

_____

16.2 Freezing Water and Magnets

4. Record the temperature every day this week on the chart below.

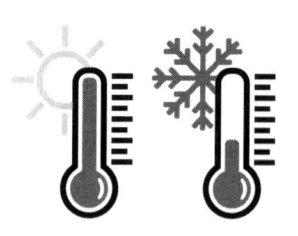

Weekly Weather Chart

Day	Temperature	Rainy, Sunny, Cloudy, Snowy, Clear

16.2 Freezing Water and Magnets Next Page

5. Draw a picture of your iron filings experiment.

6. What does the magnet do with the items below?

- paper clip
- glass jar
- screws
- nails
- silver fork

16.2 Freezing Water and Magnets

7. Find your own items. What does the magnet do with them?

☐	_____
☐	_____
☐	_____
☐	_____
☐	_____
☐	_____
☐	_____

8. Do magnets always attract objects?

   _____

   _____

9. When you completed the iron filings experiment you saw a magnetic field on the paper plate? What is a magnetic field?

   _____

   _____

   _____

57   16.2 Freezing Water and Magnets

SCIENCE

Thunder and Lightning

Name: _____

1. In the box below, draw a picture of thunder and lightning.

Draw

17.1 Thunder and Lightning

2. Lightning is a big flash of electricity, and thunder is the sound that the lightning makes. Why do you see lightning before you see thunder?

3. Draw a picture of a rainbow.

Draw

4. There are 7 colors in a rainbow. List them below and color in the boxes?

5. Draw a picture from the story.

17.1 Thunder and Lightning

Animals and Weather Change

Name: _____

1. In the boxes below, draw pictures of animals and where they live in warm weather and cold weather.

Warm Weather Home Animal: _____	Cold Weather Home
⟷	Draw

Warm Weather Home Animal: _____	Cold Weather Home
⟷	Draw

17.2 Animals and Weather Change Next Page

Warm Weather Home	Cold Weather Home
Animal: _____	

⟷

Draw

Warm Weather Home	Cold Weather Home
Animal: _____	

⟷

Draw

17.2 Animals and Weather Change

2. Draw pictures of what animals eat in both warm and cold seasons.

Warm Season Food ⟷	Cold Season Food
Animal: _____	

Draw

Warm Season Food ⟷	Cold Season Food
Animal: _____	

Draw

Warm Season Food ⟷ Cold Season Food

Animal: _____

Draw

Warm Season Food ⟷ Cold Season Food

Animal: _____

Draw

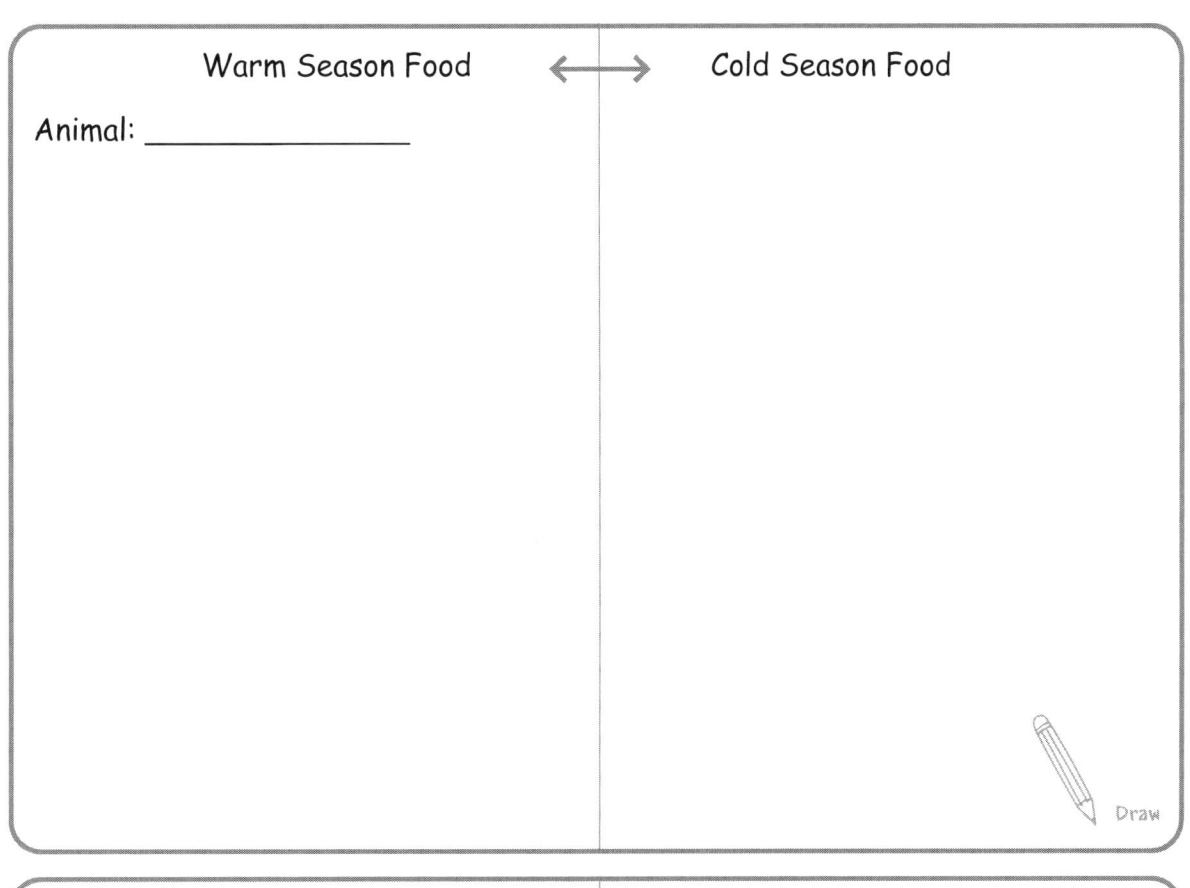

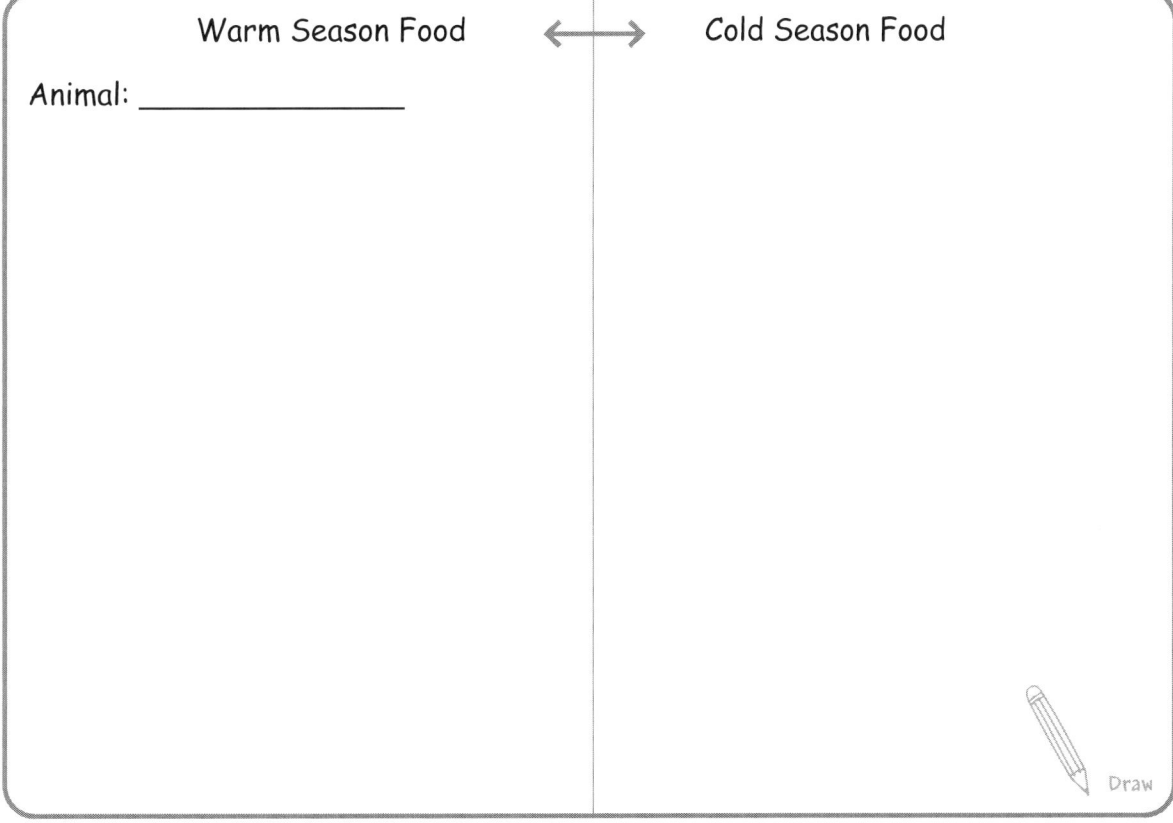

17.2 Animals and Weather Change

SCIENCE

Weather Extremes

Name: _____

1. In the box below, draw a picture of a tornado passing over a house or through a town.

Draw

65

18.1 Weather Extremes Next Page

2. Explain the damage a tornado can do to buildings and nature.

_____
_____
_____
_____
_____
_____
_____
_____

3. In the box below, draw a picture of a hurricane passing through. Show the effect on trees and the ocean.

18.1 Weather Extremes

4. Explain what a hurricane is, how it forms, and the damage it can do on land.

_____

_____

_____

_____

_____

5. In the box below, draw a picture of a blizzard on your street or someplace you've been.

Draw

18.1 Weather Extremes Next Page

6. What must happen in order for a snowstorm to be called a blizzard?

18.1 Weather Extremes

SCIENCE

Compare Environments

Name: _____

1. In the box below, draw a picture illustrating a **jungle** environment.

Draw

69   18.2 Compare Environments   Next Page

2. In the box below, draw a picture of a **desert**.

Draw

3. In the box below, draw a picture of a **polar** region.

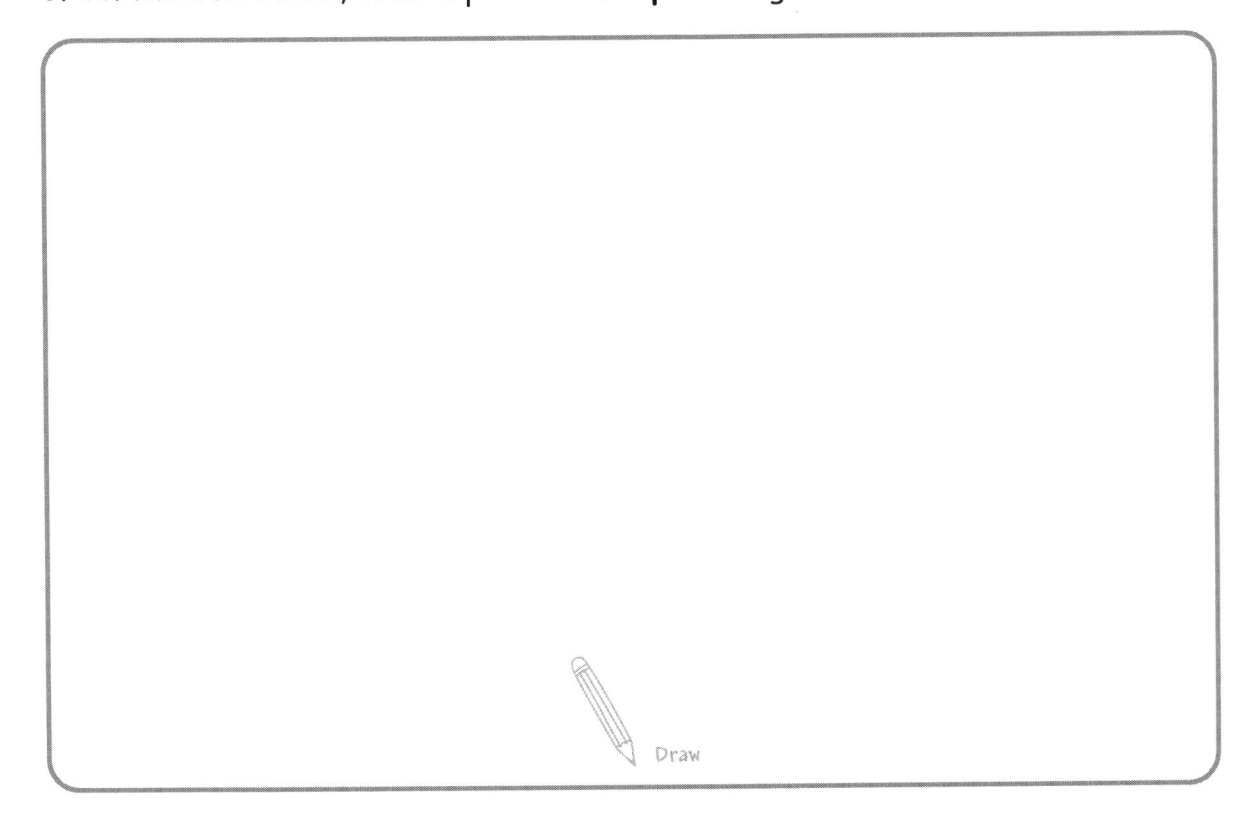

Draw

18.2 Compare Environments

4. Which region is a thick forest with lots of plants, trees and animals?

5. Which environment is known as Earth's frigid zone?

6. Which region is a large, extremely dry area of land with sparse vegetation?

7. Draw a picture of your special tree as you see it now.

[Draw]

8. Examine your chosen tree carefully. Has anything changed since you last visited it? How has it changed?

_____

_____

_____

_____

18.2 Compare Environments